HOW TO BUILD A BASIC TYPESETTING SYSTEM

HOW TO BUILD A BASIC TYPESETTING SYSTEM

Professor Michael L. Kleper

Associate Professor
Rochester Institute of Technology
National Technical Institute for the Deaf

Illustrated by
James Veatch
Assistant Professor
Rochester Institute of Technology
National Technical Institute for the Deaf

Published by the
Graphic Arts Research Center
Rochester Institute of Technology

in cooperation with
Graphic Dimensions

OTHER BOOKS BY MICHAEL KLEPER

Understanding Phototypesetting

Positive Film Make-up

Phototypesetting at a Glance

Graphic Arts Pen Techniques

Practical Control of Phototypographic
Quality (media package)

Elementary Phototypesetting Systems
Concepts (media package)

Available from:

Graphic Dimensions
25 Beekman Place
Rochester, NY 14620

Published by the Graphic Arts Research Center
Rochester Institute of Technology
One Lomb Memorial Drive
Rochester, NY 14623
In cooperation with Graphic Dimensions
25 Beekman Place
Rochester, NY 14620

ISBN #0-89938-002-6
Library of Congress #79-53427

Contents

I. "What are the present phototype-setting options?"

II. "What functions does a photo-typesetter perform?"

Exhibits

Appendices

Foreword

Sometime in the 1970's we crossed the divide between craft and automation in the use of typesetting. Skill levels were lowered coincident with the cost/performance reduction of the entire electronics industry, of which typesetting is now a sub-segment. The result was a simpler, cheaper "mousetrap" and the world beat a path to typesettings' door.

We are about to enter the 1980's and the plethora of possibilities for typesetting implementation has run rampant. The number of alternatives can overwhelm the prudent investigator. **Enter Mike Kleper**. His books, monographs, and other permanent graffiti are truly treasure maps to guide you through the unchartered depths of typesetting technology.

This present book is an interactive tool that can reduce your alternatives, narrow your choices, and pretty much pinpoint your selection. It will also enhance your understanding, expand your consciousness, and broaden your horizon. Where else can you get reduced, narrowed, pin-pointed, enhanced, expanded, and broadened in one place?

Here. Now. With love, from Mike.

FRANK J. ROMANO
Salem, New Hampshire

I.

"What are the present phototype-setting options?"

Typesetting has long been characterized both as a skill and as a technology associated with the printing trades. Indeed, it remains as a vital and integral part of the graphic arts industry. Yet, on a daily basis, more and more non-printing people are becoming involved in setting their own type. There are many reasons for this: the ease of operating these new machines, their compatibility with other standard operations, such as offset lithography and word processing, their reasonable prices, and a whole list of other advantages.

Choosing from the vast assortment of phototypesetters, keyboards, terminals, interfaces, and peripherals is a confusing task. It is the objective of this section to clarify the options open to those people unfamiliar with typesetting and to provide a direction for bringing phototypesetting into an organization.

Basic Functions

The process of converting words into photographically composed type may be accomplished in a number of ways. However the machine/people mix is concocted, there are certain characteristic functions which must be fulfilled by any phototypesetting system. First, there must be a means of translating human intelligence into a form which machines will understand. This may mean producing a recorded or electronic medium which is both machine and human readable, such as a specially prepared typewritten page, or one which is only machine readable, such as a magnetic disk. Translation may also be direct, whereby no medium is produced, and the typesetter responds directly to the electronic impulses from each key depression.

Second, there must be a way of inputting typographic descriptors, such as point size, typeface, line measure (length), and line spacing (space between lines), as well as other significant functions. To do this, there is usually a distinct code or series of instructions which are used to direct the phototypesetter to blend the given ingredients to produce the required result. The number of typographic codes (similar or dissimilar) is usually in direct proportion to the complexity of work being produced; that is, the more involved the composition, the more codes required to direct the machine to produce it.

Third, there must be a device which can be driven to photographically produce the specified characters in the specified arrangement. By so saying, we are cautioning that not all phototypesetters are capable of, nor suitable for, producing all varieties of work. Straight text, tabular matter, multiple columns, mathematical and statistical formulae, ruled forms, display advertisements, and many other categories of work all have distinct requirements which can best be served, and sometimes only be served, by the selection of the appropriate phototypesetter.

The Direct Route

An input keyboard, whether on a typewriter or typesetter, basically performs the same task. It transforms the depression of a keycap into an electronic signal and, in some cases, a visible image. Until machines can be built to convert speech and handwriting into forms recognizable by typesetting devices, there will continue to be the inescapable process of inputting by keyboard.

There are large segments of typewriter and typesetter keyboard layouts which are alike. These are the alpha (alphabet) and numeric (figure) keys, or for short, "alphanumerics." The alphanumeric characters occupy the same locations on both kinds of keyboard, and so anyone with typing proficiency can be trained to operate a phototypesetter keyboard.

It became obvious early in the development of mechanized typesetters (1830 and beyond) that the keyboard should be integrated into the design of the typesetter itself. Although the keyboard may certainly be located apart from the typesetting unit, as we will see later, there are valid reasons for not always doing so. First, when the keyboard is a built-in part of the phototypesetter, a single operator controls the entire typesetting function. One operator keyboards, makes all machine settings and adjustments, and usually processes (develops) the output. With the typesetter responding to each keystroke at the time it is struck, the operator may retain the privilege of deciding at which point lines should be ended, or words hyphenated. The operator also maintains immediate control over the fitting of character combinations, and the copyfitting of headlines, run-arounds, and mixed face and size composition.

The control which the operator exercises is the result of the typesetting machine calculating the total number of units of space that keyed characters will require on a line (we will explain how later). The machine then indicates with an audible and/or visual signal that it has tallied one line's worth of characters. Line ending information is quite useful, and keyboards which are capable of supplying such information are termed, appropriately, "counting keyboards."

Second, when the keyboard is a part of the typesetter, the cost of the single device is usually lower than if the components were separated. This is fairly obvious since not only would cabinetry and electronics need to be duplicated if the keyboard was removed, but some means of communicating across the distance of separation would also have to be devised.

Phototypesetters which have self-contained keyboards are classified as "direct input" or "direct entry" machines. They comprise a large segment of today's phototypesetting market, due not only to their relatively low prices and ease of operation, but also to their modular engineering. Modularity means that compatible functional components, such as record/playback units, off-line keyboards, and editing terminals may be added as the need arises. In this way, the growth of the phototypesetting system follows the needs of the user in a somewhat controllable manner.

Direct entry phototypesetters have certain inherent limitations which can only be overcome by expanding the system. The primary limitation is that the speed of the typesetter, in terms of the number of characters it will flash in any given span of time, is dependent upon the speed at which the operator can keyboard. In most cases, the phototypesetter can set type at a rate more than twice as fast as the operator can type. For example, an operator inputting at sixty words per minute: each word is equal to five characters plus one space, the input rate is 360 keystrokes per minute (60 × 6). A conservative phototypesetter speed might be twenty-five lines per minute.* If each line contains thirty characters, then the machine is capable of producing 750 characters per minute (25 × 30). The typesetter will also remain idle at any time that the operator is away from the machine, either on breaks, vacation, or out sick.

When the workload reaches a point where it is no longer feasible for a lone operator to produce it all, then a portion of the unused machine speed can be tapped by locating an additional keyboard away from the phototypesetter. This keyboard (and there may be more than one, depending upon the capability of the typesetter to support more) is not connected to the main machine. Instead, its keystrokes are recorded on either a paper or magnetic medium for storage. In order for the phototypesetter to be able to "read" this media, it must be equipped with an appropriate playback device.

In this configuration, the phototypesetter supports two operators, although not simultaneously. While one operator keyboards directly, the other keyboards away from the machine, or "off-line." The media produced off-line will be processed at times

*25 newspaper lines per minute, 11 pica measure of approximately 30 characters.

when the typesetter is not under the control of the direct-entry operator.

There are a variety of off-line keyboards, and they fall into three major categories. First, the keyboard may be "counting" or "noncounting." As stated before, a counting keyboard provides an indication if a given number of characters will fit on a line, or when there are a sufficient number of characters to end a line. For a keyboard to be able to count, it must have a means of storing unit value information (widths) for each and every character of each and every typeface (font) which the phototypesetter is using.

Second, the keyboard may be "visual" or "blind." There are many visual indicators available to aid the operator by indicating his or her present location in the stream of text, and by displaying erroneous characters and codes for correction. The size of the display, comprised of either light emitting diodes (LED), or a cathode ray tube (CRT) may be from a single character, up to many lines. The absence of all visual indicators renders the keyboard "blind," and while blind keyboarding is known to be faster for straight text (since the operator is not distracted by the display), it makes locating errors difficult.

Third, is the category of devices wherein errors can be corrected and major alterations to copy can be executed—"editing" keyboards. An editing keyboard, usually called a "visual display terminal" (VDT), or "tube," permits an operator to review previously keyboarded material and to add or delete any part, from single characters up to entire sections. The editing keyboard may also be used as a vehicle for inputting original copy and then reviewing it before sending it to the typesetting machine. The direct entry keyboard may also make use of the editing capabilities of the VDT by adding a record unit to capture keystrokes on a similar paper or magnetic medium. This extends the capabilities of the direct entry keyboard, not only by adding editing power, but also by providing a means of storing keyboarded information and serving as a back-up for typeset material which is lost, misplaced, or damaged.

Editing terminals have done much to enhance the efficiency and productivity of phototypesetting in general. So much so, that some machine manufacturers have replaced the limited capability direct-entry keyboard with the more powerful editing terminal. The result is a machine which looks like a direct-entry phototypesetter with a CRT, but differs in one important respect: the keyboarding and typesetting functions can occur independent of one another. This means that while the typesetter is setting job "A" (at its optimum speed), the operator may be keyboarding job "B." No longer must the typesetter follow the operator on a line-by-line basis. This also makes off-line keyboard operators more productive, since some machines of this kind will accept off-line input even while the phototypesetter keyboard operator is inputting.

Exhibit 1. Plus & Minus of Direct-Entry Phototypesetting

1. Complete operator control.
2. End-of-line decision making.
3. Automatic justification (equal right and left margins).
4. Relative low cost.
5. Modularity (on some machine lines).
6. Operable off-line (in some cases).
7. Single line correction keys common.
8. Floor space equivalent of an office desk or smaller.

1. Machine productivity limited by productivity of a single operator.
2. Hyphenation usually attainable only by operator decision (some people may consider this an advantage due to the lack of automatic hyphenation program reliability).
3. Relatively slow typesetting speeds.
4. Once the return key is hit the line(s) can not be recalled for correction.
5. Models lacking record/playback are subject to multiple rekeyboardings if original typesetting is erroneous, damaged, or lost.
6. Limited expansion (just buy more units).

The Reading Machine

Much of the material which is earmarked for typesetting passes through the operator's hands in typewritten form. Certain typewriters, using changeable type-elements, can, with minor modifications, be used to produce copy which can be used as input to a phototypesetter, without the need to rekeyboard. This process is accomplished by using machines called "Optical Character Recogition" (OCR) readers, which can scan properly prepared typewritten sheets and convert the typewritten characters and symbols into electronic signals and codes recognizable by the phototypesetter.

OCR reduces the most time-consuming and costly segment of the typesetting operation, namely, inputting, by eliminating redundant keyboarding. It does so using relatively inexpensive keyboards (typewriters) and the same typists who would normally prepare pages for rekeyboarding.

Since the typewriter is such a ubiquitous machine, its potential as a typesetting input device exists even within relatively small businesses. Likewise, the skills required of an OCR typist are little more than what is required of a competent office typist. While the cost of the OCR machine may rival the cost of the phototypesetter itself, it is able to support a host of keyboards, and therefore, the per keyboard cost of an OCR installation is typically much less than by other methods.

OCR machines are used in one of two ways. First, the device may stand alone. The pages it reads are converted into coded punched paper tape which is physically carried to the phototypesetter reader. A visual display of some sort may be added at this point to intercept tapes before running them on the typesetter, or for correcting previously run tapes. Second, the OCR machine may be wired on-line to the phototypesetter with no intermediate produced. The advantage of the former is that it permits additional editing prior to typesetting and produces a clean (error free) tape which may be retained for later use. The advantage of the latter is that it eliminates media handling altogether.

Exhibit 2. Plus & Minus of OCR

+	−
1. Elimination of rekeyboarding.	1. OCR devices are relatively expensive (relative to the cost of the typesetter).
2. Use of most typewriters for input means low per/keyboard cost.	
3. Use of typists as input operators.	2. Use of special codes may reduce operator speed.
4. Minimum operator training needed.	
5. Completely visual, hard copy proof.	3. A typewriter gives no typographic end-of-line information (non-counting).
6. Complete typographic control with no specialized keys.	
7. High reader/keyboard ratio.	4. Complex matter, tabular, advertising, mathematical, and statistical composition may not be easily set.
8. OCR may stand alone or be on-line.	
9. Document preparation may take place on or off-site. Authors might do their own inputting.	5. Limited correcting and editing.
10. Machines having automatic page feeders can be left virtually unattended.	

A Commodity of Options

Fundamentally, it is the location, kind, and number of keyboards which determines the characteristic operation of any phototype-setting system. In more precise terms, it is the relationship of the input device(s) [keyboard(s)] to the output device (photo unit) which determines how the system components and their operator(s) will function and interact. There are many ways in which the input/output, or I/O, can be configured to perform similar tasks, and so the selection of a particular arrangement must be made with consideration to all or some of the following:

1. **Present needs—** What is required to produce today's workload?
   - a. typesetting speed
   - b. number of sizes on-line
   - c. number of typefaces on-line
   - d. range of point sizes
   - e. maximum line length
   - f. tabbing capability
   - g. hyphenation method and accuracy
   - h. record/playback
   - i. availability of special characters/symbols
   - j. typographic controls
   - k. line spacing increments/range
   - l. correction methods
   - m. revisions and editing
   - n. type library

2. **Capital constraints—** What will it cost? What will it save?

3. **Machine utilization—** Will the system be kept busy?

4. **Operator availability—** Who will operate it? With what skills? How much training?

5. **Job characteristics—** Can and/or should all/some jobs be done in-house?

6. **Required turnaround—** Can the system respond to specific time limitations?

7. **Organizational commitment—** Is there widespread support for the system to succeed?

8. **Channels of communication**—Can information to be typeset be efficiently funneled into the system?
9. **Compatibility of vendors' components**—Will devices from different manufacturers work together?
10. **System support**—How many people? How much supervision?
11. **Vendor support**—Can one vendor supply all components? How about parts and service?
12. **Back-up**—What if the system breaks down?
13. **Alternate sources of input**—Can/should the company computer, WP system, interface to typesetter?
14. **Future needs**—What will be required of the system in 3, 5, or 10 years?
    a. increased speed/decreased turnaround
    b. multiple output devices
    c. mass storage and retention of information
    d. input at point of entry
    e. expandability of existing hardware

We will deal with many of these items in more detail later, but for now it is only necessary to recognize two things. First, that there are many ways to get information into a phototypesetter, and second, that understanding what your specific needs are will help to assure that the system you select will best meet your requirements.

Up to this point, we have described almost all of the components which are needed to put together a wide variety of systems. The direct-entry phototypesetter, as we have seen, is a system unto itself, but some models may be expanded to accept input from off-line sources. Off-line keyboards may be any combination of counting/non-counting, blind or visual. Editing capability may be built into a direct-entry phototypesetter or may take the form of a free standing terminal, which may be connected to a system in a number of ways. We have also seen that certain typewriters may be used for input when interfaced with an OCR device.

A new kind of office typewriter, having many of the capabilities of a visual display terminal with a magnetic record/playback, has appeared in recent years, under the name of "word processor." Word processing (WP) eliminates redundant keyboarding by recording original keystrokes for eventual revision. When changes to a document are made, only the revisions need to be keyboarded, other sections are played back unchanged. The product is a cleanly typed document which may remain in magnetic storage for future use. One rapidly growing use is the further processing of the magnetic media into phototypeset output. Appropriate interfaces are presently available to interpret magnetic word processing cards, cassettes, and disks into codes which can drive a phototypesetter.

An organization having word processing equipment installed already has a major component of a phototypesetting system. It has a front-end device having editing capability, record/playback, and hard copy (for proofreading). Here is a powerful off-line keyboard on which the bulk of the typesetting operation, namely input, can be effectively produced.

A System of Systems

The first distinction in describing a phototypesetting system is the relationship of the keyboard to the photo unit. Symbolically,the keyboard may be represented as physically attached to the photo unit like this:

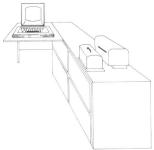

or standing alone.

A photo unit which stands alone requires some method of accepting the media which is produced at some remote location, and it may be symbolized like this:

All editing devices have CRT screens, and may be so diagramed:

The other pieces of equipment discussed are the typewriter:

the word processor:

an interface device:

and the OCR scanner.

When devices are connected by a cable:

they are on-line. When devices are not on-line (or totally on-line) they commonly communicate by use of a medium such as OCR scannable copy,

OCR Documents

perforated tape,

magnetic tape cassette,

or magnetic floppy disk.

Any system, no matter how ingenious, is meaningless without people — people to generate the input, run it through the typesetter, process the output, layout pages, and reproduce copies. How well a system works depends much more on the people that interact with it than on the actual equipment (assuming it functions as it should).

Information enters the typesetting cycle in either written (typed or hand) or oral (tape recorded) form. It leaves the phototypesetter as black images on white paper or clear film, photographic or otherwise.

Depending upon the size of the system, the complexity, urgency, and length of the work, it may require many people to keyboard, to edit, to monitor the photo unit, to process the output, to proofread, and to keyboard corrections; or it may require only a single operator to perform all functions.

Even the smallest system, the simplest direct-entry phototypesetter, may fulfill all of the diverse requirements of an organization, while a large powerful system may be mismatched to the needs of its users. Putting together the components of a system is no easy task. It is sometimes a compromise between funds and feasibility, and availability and suitability. But, regardless of the difficulties in specifying equipment, it is foolhardy to even try without understanding the needs of the organization. (See Exhibit 3).

Exhibit 3. Examples of System Configurations

System Description	System Configuration	System Characteristics

Direct-entry: self-contained keyboard/photo unit

1	2	3	4	5	6	7	8	9
s	s	s	n	n	y	s	n	s

Direct-entry with off-line keyboard: addition of record/playback on photo unit. Multiple operators

1	2	3	4	5	6	7	8	9
y	n	y	y	y	y	s	n	s

Direct-entry with off-line editing: multiple operators

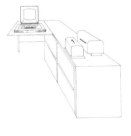

1	2	3	4	5	6	7	8	9
y	y	y	y	y	y	s	n	s

System Description	**System Configuration**	**System Characteristics**

4. Stand-alone I/O: single operator

1	2	3	4	5	6	7	8	9
y	n	y	n	y	n	s	s	s

5. Stand-alone I/O with VDT: multiple operators

1	2	3	4	5	6	7	8	9
y	y	y	y	y	n	s	s	s

6. Stand-alone I/O with multiple keyboards: multiple operators (speed of photo unit limits the number of keyboards it can support)

1	2	3	4	5	6	7	8	9
y	n	y	y	y	n	s	s	s

**System
Description**

**System
Configuration**

**System
Characteristics**

Stand-alone I/O with mul-
tiple keyboards and single
VDT

1 2 3 4 5 6 7 8 9
y y y y n s s s

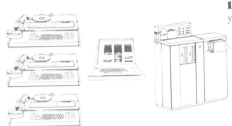

On-line photo unit to
clustered VDTs: VDTs on-
line to computer, photo
unit as an output device

1 2 3 4 5 6 7 8 9
y y y y n y s s s

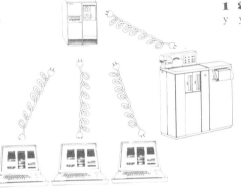

On-line OCR to photo unit

1 2 3 4 5 6 7 8 9
y n n y n y s s y

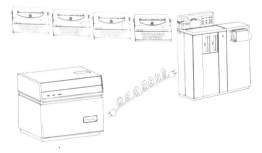

10. On-line WP interface
    with off-line keyboard

1 2 3 4 5 6 7 8 9
y n* y y y n y n n

y = yes
n = no
s = sometimes

1. Expandable
2. Editing
3. Record/Playback
4. Multiple input operators
5. Off-line operation
6. On-line operation
7. Interface with WP
8. Interface with computer
9. Interface with OCR

*editing functions of word processor for media so created.

18

II.

"What functions does a phototypesetter perform?"

Typographic Functions

The word "type" is derived from the Latin **typus** meaning "image," and the Greek **typos** meaning "impression" or "model." Metal type characters, as we have known them through the history of printing, are individual rectangular blocks having a relief image across one endmost surface. In order for the character to be readable and useful, its character surface must be inked and impressed against paper. The type itself serves to impress the image it carries on its surface directly to the printing substrate. This printing process is called "letterpress," and it was the dominant printing process from Gutenberg up to the 1960's. Although letterpress printing and metal typesetting systems are not extinct, they have given way to the offset lithographic printing process. "Offset" (sometimes called "litho," "lithography," or "photo offset") requires type characters composed on a flat surface, usually photographic paper or film.* For this reason and for a very long list of others,† phototypesetting has become the dominant method of typesetting today.

*Reproduction proofs, which are carefully printed impressions from metal type, can be used to satisfy the composition requirements of offset lithography.

†See Michael L. Kleper: UNDERSTANDING PHOTOTYPESETTING, Philadelphia, (1975), pp. 118-119.

Metal typesetting has exerted a considerable impact on how we use phototypesetting. It is apparent that much of the metal terminology remains, to the bewilderment and confusion of those unfamiliar with its use. We will begin unraveling the mystery by defining a few terms which are used throughout this book.

Type font. A type font is the collection of alphanumeric characters, punctuation, and special characters and symbols of one particular type design, in one particular size.

Bookman Light Italic w/Swash

abcdefghijklmnopqrstuvwxyz

ABCDEFGHIJKLMNOPQRSTUVWXYZ

1234567890 1234567890

e-fihfikmno-pqr t

A ABBCDEFGHIJKLMNOPQRR

STUVVWWWXYZ

(&C&.,:;!?'""--·*$¢%/£)

Type font master. A font master is the form in which the font is held for use on the phototypesetting machine. It may be a disk, strip, matrix grid, or electronically digitized.

Type size. Type size is generally judged as the vertical measurement in points (72 points = 1 inch) between the uppermost limit of an upward reaching character (ascender) such as a **b**, **d**, or **f**, and the lowermost limit of a downward projecting character (descender), such as a **g**, **j**, or **p**.

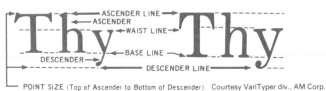

POINT SIZE (Top of Ascender to Bottom of Descender)   Courtesy VariTyper div., AM Corp.

20

Typeface. The typeface is the description of the characters in a type font in terms of its design, style, or distinguishing "character"istics. Some common typeface classifications follow:

Roman. Upright characters (as opposed to italic characters which slant to the right) which have serifs (ending strokes) at their extremities.

NAPOLEON'S GENIUS

Sans Serif. Characters which do not have serifs.

THE MERCHANT OF VENICE

Script. Joined characters resembling ornate penmanship.

Italian Engravings

Blackletter. Bold ornamented designs with heavy angular serifs. Also collectively, although erroneously, called Old English.

Music washes
away from the soul
the dust of
everyday life

Modern. Mechanically constructed, with heavy stems and light serifs.

PARK RIDING ACADEMY

Square Serif. Characters with prominent square-shaped serifs.

Biped

Decorative (or Display). Type designs which do not fit in any previous category and which have unique ornamentation or other distinctive features.

Japanette   Kismet

Houghton   Karnac

ROMANTIQUE   Lariat

Type Characters. Type characters are the individual letter, figure, punctuation, and special character shapes. They are the smallest functional units in typesetting, and aside from the alphanumerics, may differ substantially from font-to-font in their numbers of different characters (font size). The array of characters found in a particular font is called the "character repertoire" or "character set."

Type Specimen. A type specimen is a printed sample of a particular typeface shown for the purpose of making an appropriate selection.

Typesetter. The typesetter is either the person who, or the machine which, sets type.

Typography. Typography is the process (sometimes considered an art) of selecting, arranging, and using type.

Typesetting (Composition, Typographic Composition). Typesetting is the assembly of typographic characters into larger functional units, i.e. words, sentences, paragraphs, pages, chapters, books, and volumes.

The Unit System

Long before printing evolved as a mass medium, reproductions of scholarly works and church matter were meticulously hand copied by scribes. Paper was so highly valued that scribes had to fit as many characters on a line as possible. Two traditions evolved from this activity. First, characters receive an amount of horizontal space relative to their width, that is a "W" receives proportionately more horizontal space than a "j." Second, all lines are of the same length. These characteristics were adopted by Gutenberg so that the mechanical printing process could mimic the manual art of the scribes.

Unlike an office typewriter, which gives each character an identical share of horizontal space, a phototypesetter composes characters one-beside-another, with no obvious spatial separation. The advantages of variably spaced typeset characters over monospaced typewritten characters are:

1. Typeset characters conserve space. Typesetting may reduce page space requirements by 40-60% or more.

2. Typeset characters are easier to read; their character and word shapes are more distinctive and therefore more easily scanned by the reader's eyes.

3. Typeset characters look better. The photographic process gives considerable flexibility in the letter design, character weight (thicks and thins), and size.

The proper fitting together of characters is a very conscientious task for anyone setting type. The characters are assigned width values by typesetting machine manufacturers, and some reference to these values should be available to every keyboard operator.

Width values are assigned in units. The units are determined on the basis of the **em space**, a square of space measuring the same point size on all four sides. The widest character in a font, the capital "W," for example, is usually as wide as the em space. Machine manufacturers divide the em into a number of equal vertical slices, usually 18, but up to over 100. Each slice is called a "unit." It doesn't matter if the type size is 6 point or 72 point, there will still be the same number of units to the em in that one system. The actual size of a 6 point unit will, however, be much smaller than a 72 point unit even though they are both members of an 18 unit system. For this reason we refer to these units as "relative units" (RU), since their true measurements are relative to their point sizes.

The actual width of characters of different sizes may be expressed by the following:

RU × Point Size = Actual Width

The unit values are useful for a number of purposes, the first of which is **justification**.

Justification

Justification is the process of setting lines of type of equal line length, or in other words, blocks of composition with equal right and left hand margins. The length of the lines are measured in picas (6 picas = 1 inch) or in picas and points (12 points = 1 pica). In order to calculate how many characters will fit on one line, say of 24 picas, it is necessary to convert the line measure into relative units. Relative units must refer to a specific point size, since the number of units in a given line length varies according to the size of type set on it. Selecting 10 point type on the 24 pica line measure gives this result:

$$24 \text{ picas} = 288 \text{ points}$$
$$1 \ 10 \text{ point em} = 18 \text{ units}$$
$$288 \text{ points} \div 10 \text{ point em} = 28.8 \text{ ems}$$
$$28.8 \text{ ems} \times 18 \text{ units/em} = \mathbf{518.4} \text{ units of 10 pt.}$$

If a smaller type size is selected it will result in more units available on the same line length. Switching to 6 point type on the 24 pica measure:

$$\text{Again, } 24 \text{ picas} = 288 \text{ points}$$
$$1 \ 6 \text{ point em} = 18 \text{ units}$$
$$288 \text{ points} \div 6 \text{ point em} = 48 \text{ ems}$$
$$48 \text{ ems} \times 18 \text{ units/em} = \mathbf{864} \text{ units of 6 pt.}$$

Conversely, a larger type size, say 14 points, will offer fewer units to the line:

$$24 \text{ picas} = 288 \text{ points}$$
$$1 \ 14 \text{ point em} = 18 \text{ units}$$
$$288 \text{ points} \div 14 \text{ point em} = 20.5 \text{ ems}$$
$$20.5 \text{ ems} \times 18 \text{ units/em} = \mathbf{369} \text{ units of 14 pt.}$$

The total unit count includes both characters and spaces needed to fill the line measure. Word spaces are usually designated by a minimum and maximum range of permissible values. When the line is keyboarded, the minimum unit space value is counted in the calculation. The keyboard operator tries to get as much on a single line as possible, keeping the word spaces to a minimum and setting the copy "tight." As the units remaining in the line measure approach zero, the operator must make decisions, such as if a word which can not entirely fit on the end of the line will be broken (hyphenated), or carried to the next line. The point in the line at which there are enough characters and spaces to justify the line, without exceeding the maximum word space, is the "justification" or "hot zone." The line may be ended at any point once the justification zone is entered, although tradition requires ending the line as close to zero as possible. Tightly set lines avoid "rivers" of white space flowing through loosely set composition. Any units short of zero are added between the line's wordspaces (and sometimes letterspaces) to "space-out" the line to fill the measure.

The formula for determining the actual value of each word space is:

$$\frac{\text{Total Line Length} - \text{Total of Characters/Spaces}}{\text{Number of Word Spaces}} = \begin{array}{c}\text{Value of each} \\ \text{Word space for} \\ \text{Justification}\end{array}$$

Letterspacing

Letterspacing is the activity of adding space between characters. It is practiced for two reasons. First, it is a function of taste, extending the space between characters (usually capitals) at the judgment of the typographer, to improve their appearance. Its objective is to give each character a sovereign, yet equal looking space, without destroying the readability of the word(s). For example:

LIBRARY

LIBRARY

Second, it is a machine function (if so instructed) which automatically adds space between characters to take-up excess space in a line so as to avoid unusually large wordspaces. By so doing, however, the character fit, and therefore readability, of the letterspaced words usually suffers. Here are some examples of excessively letterspaced lines:

I t w a s l i k e t h e c h i l l i n g f r o s t t h a t
d r i v e s i t s w a y u p t h e s u r f a c e o f a
b r o k e n p a n e o f g l a s s . R e a c h i n g w i t h
i t s b o n y c r y s t a l f i n g e r s t o t h e e d g e
o f t w i l i g h t . N o w h e r e c o u l d t h e

Kerning

Kerning is the function of reducing space between characters. Like letterspacing, it serves two purposes: one aesthetic, one functional. Aesthetic kerning is used to fit characters together according to their shape relationships with adjoining characters. Functionally, removing objectionable space not only improves the readability of the word(s), but also saves space on the printed page. (This is sometimes called "negative letterspacing.")

Characters have distinctive shapes, yet the unit system tends to treat each character as a rectangular block, assigning so many fixed units of horizontal space to each. In text sizes (smaller than 14 point), the space differences in letter combinations is not noticeable; it does not interfere with the reader's rate of word scan. It is usually with display type sizes (those above 14 point) that irregularly large spaces appearing between certain letter combinations becomes unacceptable. It is in these instances that units or whole points of horizontal space are discriminately removed by the keyboard operator.

Line spacing

The vertical distance between each typeset line is the "line spacing."* It is equal to the number of points (and sometimes half-points) that the photographic material is advanced with the depression of the return key. Once the photographic material is advanced it can not be backed-up unless the phototypesetter has a "reverse leading" feature. This feature significantly extends the capability of the typesetter since it is virtually the only way that multiple-column and mathematical and statistical formulae can be set. It simplifies the composition of other kinds of work where characters in a line do not all share a common baseline.

Each phototypesetting machine has a range of line spacing values built-in. The maximum value is the largest advance of photographic material obtainable by the depression of the return key. The minimum value is the smallest increment by which the line spacing value may be increased. This increment is commonly ½ to ¼ point, but may be specified in millimeters (mm), or in fractions of an inch.

Some keyboards feature a secondary leading key. This is an additional operator selected value which can be used at any time in place of the primary leading or line spacing increment. It is useful to separate blocks of copy, such as paragraphs, heads, or subheads, or for repeatedly used line spacing values different from the primary.

6 point type / 6 points of line space

Printing from moveable type was not so much an invention as an evolution. The printing of pictures from incised blocks of wood gradually gave way to the inclusion of a limited number of lines of text. Although it seemed practical to print text along with illustrations it was still an uneconomical expenditure of time and skill.

6 point type / 7 points of line space

Printing from moveable type was not so much an invention as an evolution. The printing of pictures from incised blocks of wood gradually gave way to the inclusion of a limited number of lines of text. Although it seemed practical to print text along with illustrations it was still an uneconomical expenditure of time and skill.

6 point type / 8 points of line space

Printing from moveable type was not so much an invention as an evolution. The printing of pictures from incised blocks of wood gradually gave way to the inclusion of a limited number of lines of text. Although it seemed practical to print text along with illustrations it was still an uneconomical expenditure of time and skill.

6 point type / 9 points of line space

Printing from moveable type was not so much an invention as an evolution. The printing of pictures from incised blocks of wood gradually gave way to the inclusion of a limited number of lines of text. Although it seemed practical to print text along with illustrations it was still an uneconomical expenditure of time and skill.

*In metal typesetting the spatial separation of lines was accomplished by inserting thin lead strips called "leads" between the lines. Some systems still use the term "leading" (led-ing) in place of "line spacing".

Line Length

Unlike a typewriter carriage which can accept documents of almost any reasonable width, a phototypesetter has an overall maximum line length. A more or less standard line length is 45 picas (7½"), although some sophisticated machines go up to 100 picas (16⅔"). The 45 pica measure is popular because it relates well to the standard width of business forms and correspondence, namely the 8½" dimension of an 8½" x 11" sheet. Most phototypesetters also accept a variety of photographic material widths to conserve on material when the full width size is not needed.*

Point Sizes

There is relatively little choice in the character size available on office typewriters. Therefore, the same size characters must be used for headings and footnotes as is used for the main text. Phototypesetters, on the other hand, are able to set a number of sizes, from a few to many dozen. The low range of size usually begins with 6 point type, typically used for the fine print on business forms, or for portions of business cards. Although it is possible to have sizes on a machine at each point or half-point increment, it is not the usual case, so we can skip a size here and there. 8 or 9 point type might be used for captions under photographs or illustrations, or for section headings on business forms. This is also the typical size used for newspaper matter. 10 to 12 point type is in the text size range, used for most reading matter. Sizes above 14 are classified as display sizes. Sizes 14 to 18 point are used for headings and subheads. Sizes 24 to 30 point might be used for chapter titles, product labels, or advertisements. The largest size available on a phototypesetter is usually 36 point (½") or 72 point (1").

The number of sizes available on the machine between its smallest and largest sizes is significant for it will determine, in part, the categories of work which can, or can not, be produced. Machines which favor the smaller sizes are termed "low range," while those having a wider array of sizes are termed "high range." Although a machine may offer a high range, it may only have a few sizes within the range, so it is significant to deal both with the breadth of the range, and with the number of sizes within it.

*CAUTION: Loading photographic materials requires a leader of from several inches to one or more feet, and therefore frequent changing of material sizes may waste more material than it saves.

Tabbing

On a typewriter a "tab" is a predetermined stop used to align characters to form columns, for standardized indentions, or merely for vertical organization. On a phototypesetter the same purposes are satisfied, but the capabilities are further expanded by additional tabbing functions:*

Actual. The size of each tab is specified individually. The machine determines the overall line measure as well as the starting point of each successive tab.

Arithmetic. The machine automatically calculates the size of each tab by dividing the given line length by the number of tabs specified by the operator.

Automatic. A tab may be set at any point in a line during actual composition. This may be done to establish a beginning point for an indented block of text, for a word underline, or for copy which is to be centered below a word or group of words which are not on the center of the line measure.

Floating. This is a stored tab width which can be inserted at any time in addition to, or in place of, normal tab positions.

Multiple Justification. A basic tab-like function which repeats a small fixed line measure across a page to form equal length tab columns.

Proportional. Let's say the copy to be set appears to the operator to require twice as much space in columns one, three, and five, as in columns two, four, and six. By inputting a string of codes such as TAB 2,1,2,1,2,1, the machine would recognize that tabs 1, 3, and 5 are twice as wide as tabs 2, 4, and 6. The machine would add the parts, (2 + 1 + 2 + 1 + 2 + 1 = 9), divide the line length by that value, and multiply the result by the tab factor.

Typewriter Tabs. Each tab is of variable length and is numbered in order of its serial location from the left-hand margin.

---

*Not found on all machine models.

Typewriter tabs are fairly easy to plan since each typewritten character occupies a predictable amount of space (monospacing). The reverse is true for typesetting since line ending locations can not usually be anticipated without machine intelligence and operator judgment.

The number of tabs that can be positioned across a measure varies from machine-to-machine. If an organization has specific tabular needs which comprise a significant portion of their typesetting workload, then special attention must be paid to the tabbing capability in terms of its ease of use, complement of alternative methods, tab coding and accessing procedures, keyboard tab position indicators, and use of tabs with reverse line spacing.

Line Packing Functions

Most phototypesetters are capable of generating repetitive characters, symbols, or line segments across an entire line measure, or any segment thereof. The most common of these are the "insert rule" and "insert leader" functions. A "rule" is a printer's term for "line", and is composed of short segments exposed in series to form a continuous span, like this:

single 10 point line segment = __

10 point rule_____

6 point rule_____

24 point rule_____

72 point rule ██

A "leader" is a baseline dot, usually a period, often centered on an en space (half as wide as an em space). Its function is to "lead" the reader's eye across the page, like this:

Although horizontal lines are fairly universal, relatively few phototypesetters are capable of generating vertical rules. These are usually added by hand after the type and horizontal rules are set. The paste-up artist may use a technical drawing pen to rule directly on the typeset galley, or rule on a clear plastic overlay. Another method is to adhere graphic arts tape, available in a large variety of widths and designs, in place on the paste-up.*

Formats

Phototypesetters must literally be led by the hand when it comes to carrying out typographic instructions. Some machines are inoperable without the insertion of basic typesetting instructions. Others revert to default values when basic parameters are not inserted. In still other cases the machines use whatever values may have been left in memory from the previous job. Why is this significant?

An ordinary office typewriter has forty-four keys. The shift key preceding each, doubles the number of obtainable characters to eighty-eight. Eighty-eight characters suffices for most everyday office communications, but typesetting, offering more sophistication in type size and style, also offers more variety in the array of characters (usually ninety-six to one hundred twenty-eight), and in the functions (twenty to one hundred commands) which control them. Most type fonts typically have well over one hundred characters, which may include such things as fractions, mathematical signs, superior and inferior figures, trade and commercial marks, footnote references, small capitals, as well as other special symbols.

Rather than place many additional keys on the keyboard, the usual approach is to add an additional precedence key, called a super shift, command code, or a "flag" key. When the typesetting machine senses such a code, it is alerted to the fact that the keystrokes which follow are to be treated in a manner different from their usual shift or unshift identities.

---

* We will discuss paste-ups later.

Typographic functions, of which there are dozens, such as tab information, word space range, kerning, flash status, etc. are also inserted via the precedence key, or in some cases via special keys dedicated to frequently used functions. When the precedence key is used, the function is usually indicated by one or two letters which indicate its identity. Tab, for example, might be indicated as "tb," hyphenation program "on," might be "ho." Letters used in this manner, that is, as memory devices, are called "mnemonics," after the Greek goddess of memory, Mnenosyne. Mnenomics are easily learned and quickly recalled, and obviously expand the versatility of a keyboard considerably.

Typographic requirements may differ greatly from job-to-job, or may even be quite diverse within a single job. Here is where the concept of "format" can be applied. The word "format" has a number of meanings within a typesetting context, so we will define it as a string of codes identifying significant typographic descriptors. In this usage, the keyboard format relates directly to the page format. In a given job there may be many formats. One, for example, might be related to the handling of straight matter, another for tables, a third for headings and subheads, still another for footnotes, and so on. The format contains all of the typographic information to handle each kind of composition, and render it in its proper form on the typeset page.

If a given job is fairly complex, there will be many format changes, requiring the insertion of a lengthy string of codes on each occasion. Many phototypesetting systems have the means to store formats in memory locations, easily retrieved with no more than a few keystrokes. This technique of "stored formats," not only saves repetitive keyboarding, but also reduces the margin for error in these all-important typesetting parameters.

Keyboard Layouts

Picture in your mind a typewriter keyboard. Whatever mental image you have, be it green, gray, or black keycaps, the alphanumeric characters are all in their fixed positions. Without hesitation, a typist could make the transition from one of your cerebral typewriters to another.

A phototypesetter keyboard offers greater flexibility in meeting the specific needs of users. Therefore, there are keyboard layouts carrying the special characters most suited to newspapers, book publishers, commercial and specialty printers, scientific journal publishers, banks, international organizations, trade typographers, pennysavers, and so on.

When the phototypesetter is built, the appropriate keycaps are fitted on the keyboard. At least initially, the font which is used on the machine will correspond to the keycaps on a one-to-one basis. But the user is not restricted to using fonts which match the keyboard layout. Any font which has been made for the phototypesetter, regardless of layout, may be used. At any time, the operator must be aware of which character will flash with each key depression. Changing the keycaps is time consuming, and of dubious value since good operators rarely look at the keyboard while inputting. In instances where the keyboard layout is different from the one that the operator is accustomed to, a layout reference must be displayed within sight of the operator.

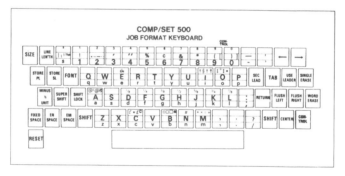

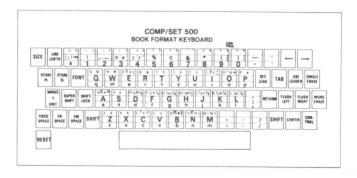

Selecting Typefaces

There is no accurate count of the number of typefaces available for all of the typesetting machines currently in use, but even a conservative estimate would put the number well into the thousands. How does one begin to choose typefaces when even a single vendor offers a staggering number of selections? The first step would be to gather samples characteristic of the kinds of work which the contemplated typesetting system will be required to produce. This is followed by a simple classification of the variety of type styles, variations, and sizes most commonly used. Before doing so, however, it's necessary to cover a little more ground.

A fundamental typeface design may undergo a series of standard modifications to extend its typographic usefulness. When variations of a typeface design are available in some or all of such forms as italic, condensed, expanded, outline, bold, shadow, backslant, light face, medium face, or any other exaggerated form, then the related designs form a "type family."

A Composite Picture of the complete GOUDY TYPE FAMILY *is here shown for the first time*

Goudy Catalogue

Goudy Catalogue Italic

Goudy Oldstyle

Goudy Italic

Goudy Cursive

GOUDY TITLE

Goudy Bold

Goudy Bold Italic

Goudy Handtooled

Goudy Handtooled Italic

Families are important because their subtle differences in design, yet overall style similarities, make their use appropriate for a wide range of work. The italic and bold forms of an upright design, for example, are especially well-suited for emphasizing important information, or to further organize textual matter for the reader. Information which would be underlined on a typewriter may be italicized on a typesetter. Similarly, words which are set in all capitals on a typewriter could be set in boldface on a typesetter. The style variations of a type design, most usually italic and/or bold, therefore serve to give an overall impression of design integrity while significantly enhancing the designer's typographic choices.

Size too plays an important part in organizing information on a reader's page. Relative size frequently relates to relative importance. A range of text (smaller than 14 points) and display (larger than 14 points) sizes of a particular typeface comprises a "type series." Theoretically, a phototypesetter, which resembles a photographic enlarger in many respects, is capable of setting any size or fractional size from a single type master. Practically, however, there are engineering and economic limitations which restrict size availability to a specific number of sizes.

With these few concepts covered it's time to take a typographic survey of the gathered samples. On a clean sheet of paper write the following categories along the top edge:

JOB N F I	SIZE(S)	TYPE CLASSIFICATION(S)	FAMILY(IES)	TYPEFACE(S) (if known)

Next, sort the samples in order of their overall importance (**I**) in terms of future in-house typesetting. Label the samples alphabetically, with the most important sample being "A." Next, list the sample order on your worksheet in column **I**, filling-in information under each heading. Sort the samples again, this time in order of the most frequently produced jobs (**F**). List the ranking in column **F**. Sort the jobs one last time in order of the absolute need to duplicate the typographic characteristics of the samples with a proposed typesetting system. List the ranking in column **N**.

Your rankings should look something like this:

N	F	I
C	B	A
A	E	B
B	D	C
E	A	D
D	C	E
F	F	F

Next, we assign consecutive ascending numbers to each letter in each column:

N	F	I
C1	B1	A1
A2	E2	B2
B3	D3	C3
E4	A4	D4
D5	C5	E5
F6	F6	F6

The overall rank score for each sample can be computed by adding its numberical rank. For example, sample "A" has a rank of 2 in column **N**, 4 in column **F**, and 1 in column **I**, for a total of 7. The complete ranking looks like this:

A - 7
B - 6
C - 9
D - 12
E - 11
F - 18

Placing the final rank order of the samples for combined overall importance (**I**), frequency (**F**), and need to duplicate (**N**) as:

F
D
E
C
A
B

If each of the rankings carries equal weight, that is, of equal importance, then the final rank serves as a good guide to the sizes and typefaces required. Individual user needs will probably require some modification to this procedure, such as adding rankings for other factors, or applying relative weights, such as **N** is twice as important as **F** and **I**.

Character Repertoire

The selection of the type sizes, typefaces, and keyboard layout (font arrangement) which are used to dress a phototypesetter, result in the array of flashable characters, that is, the character repertoire. The repertoire is calculated as the number of sizes × the number of characters in the font × the number of typefaces. Exhibit 4 shows some examples.

Exhibit 4. Character Repertoire Estimates

Machine	No. Sizes	No. of Char. Per Font	No. Faces	Char. Repert.
1	1	108	1	108
2	2	96	2	384
3	8	118	8	7552
4	5	105	4	2100
5	38	112	4	17024

III.

"How do people communicate with machines?"

Human Interfacing

Communicating with an office typewriter is direct; a one-for-one relationship of "key depressions" resulting in "character impressions." The results are immediate, visual, and tangible. The placement of characters, the limitations of line length and page depth, even the choice of typefaces (on certain typewriters) are all under the physical control of the typist. A phototypesetting machine, on the other hand, uses image-forming techniques, which by their very nature, must take place out of view. There is always a time lag between the keyboard operation (input) and the processing operation (output).

The phototypesetting machine is, of course, a much more complex device, not only in terms of hardware, but in terms of the many typographic functions it is able to perform. Directing these functions requires an operator who is able to conceptualize the finished composition before it is keyboarded; unless it is uncomplicated work, such as straight matter, or if the copy has been previously marked-up with all of the necessary codes.

Coding is the language by which the operator communicates with the machine, directing it to perform any number of different functions (see Exhibit 5). It is much more basic than computer programming (in all but large typesetting systems) and while generally easy to learn and to use, it requires training and experience to apply with a degree of professionalism.

The specifics of coding vary from machine to machine, but fundamental similarities do exist. Every typeset job has a group of at least four descriptors, called "parameters," which provide the machine with the values required to properly process the input. The parameters are like settings on a washing machine; both specify how a particular load is to be handled.

The basic parameters include the typeface, line measure, point size, and line space. Many machines have dedicated keys for inputting each of these. Once input, all characters which follow will conform to the initial parameters. Simple jobs, then, may be typeset with as few as four typographic code strings. Complex jobs, however, require frequent changes in any or all of the basic parameters, plus many additional codes. In advertising or tabular work the number of keystrokes required for codes may equal or exceed the keystrokes required for characters. (See FORMATS page 32).

Mark-up

Mark-up is the activity of specifying typographic instructions. In large installations, full-time mark-up people mark copy with the appropriate coding for submission to keyboard operators. Properly marked copy usually requires no operator intervention thereafter (for code determination, that is).

There is a great deal of variation in mark-up notation obviating any sort of mark-up standards. Some suggested mark-up codes, based on common usage are found in Exhibit 6.

Exhibit 5. Common Mnemonic Codes

Mnemonic Code	Proper Name	Meaning
SM	**S**et **M**easure	Followed by four digits. Establishes line length in picas and points.
SL	**S**et **L**inespacing	Followed by three digits. Establishes space between lines in full and fractional point increments.
P	**P**oint size	Followed by two or three (¼ size) digits. Specifies lens magnification.
F	**F**ont (**F**ace)	Followed by one, sometimes two digits. Typeface style.
TB	**T**ab	Followed by one or two digits. Establishes a tab identification number.
ST	**S**et **T**ab	Followed by four digits. Specifies distance from left margin.
IL	**I**nsert **L**eader	Fills line measure with leaders.
SO	**S**pace **O**nly	Machine escapes character units without flashing.
HO	**H**yphenation **O**n	Activates hyphenation logic program.
SU	**S**ubtract **U**nit	Moves (kerns) character which follows it one unit closer.
EL	**E**nd **L**ine	Ends line, as does "return," but inhibits line space value.

Exhibit 6. Common Mark-up Designations

Function	Designation	Meaning
Line measure	X as in "X18"	line length in picas
Line spacing	/ as /"12"	line spacing in points
Reverse lead	RL	reverse film transport
Size	/ as in "10/" circled #	size in points lens size
Typeface	T.R. 6	initials, ex. Times Roman serial location in mach.
Justified copy	Just.	set to full measure
Quadded copy	QL [RR QR] QC] [Ctr	quad left ragged right quad right quad center
Typeface variations	Ital. underline bld xbld cond	Italic underline bold extra bold condensed
Indention	1M 3M N T KX	one em indent three em indent en space indent thin space indent kern "x" units
Kill width	Ø W	inhibit character width
Kill flash	Ø F	inhibit character flash
Tab	T	tab number

Correction Techniques

The input process is composed of a great number of repetitions of a single activity—namely the depression of key caps. The serial order in which the keys are depressed as well as the proper selection of required characters and codes account for the degree of inputting accuracy.

Most contemporary keyboards have a high degree of reliability, usually not exceeding one electronic or mechanical error in 30,000 key depressions. Human reliability is much less, however. There is evidence that the lowest human error rate is between one to ten errors per 6000 keystrokes.

All input is composed of keystrokes—keystrokes for typographic images, and keystrokes for the functions which control their appearance. Incorrect character selections result in typographic errors, or "typos," but incorrect function codes can result, depending upon the typesetting system, in more serious consequences.

The most common typographic errors include "transpositions," wherein adjacent characters appear in reverse order; "omissions," wherein characters, words, or entire lines are missing; and "duplications," wherein extra characters, words, or lines are present.

The commission of typographic errors is an unpredictable yet constant part of the typesetting process. Many factors work to influence the error rate and they are associated with the job, the operator, the keyboard, and the environment.*

The ease by which errors are corrected is predicated upon the ease by which they are identified, and sometimes by the proximity, in time, to their commission.

Every keyboard is built with some correction capability, from rubbing out a single character, to transposing entire paragraphs. Regardless of the sophistication of the keyboard, there are a number of possibilities regarding when and how corrections will be made. (See Exhibit 7).

*For more information see "Practical Control of Phototypographic Quality," Michael L. Kleper, Graphic Dimensions (Rochester, 1978), pp. 3-6.

Exhibit 7. Methods of Error Correction

System Configuration	Correction Sequence	Correction Techniques
1. off-line, blind keyboard/ typesetter	before typesetting	minimally by character erase optionally by word erase, line erase
2. off-line, blind keyboard/ VDT/typesetter	before or after typesetting	correction routines (as in #1) at time of keyboarding and before or after typesetting on editing terminal
3. VDT/typesetter	before typesetting	use of VDT for initial input— several editing and correcting functions.
4. direct entry	before typesetting	if error is identified before line is sent to photo unit all or part may be erased
	after typesetting	if unit has record/playback and errors are major, the job may require rekeyboarding. If unit has no R/P and errors are minor, corrections may be reset and pasted-in.
5. word processor/interface typesetter	before typesetting	editing and correcting capabilities of specific WP unit
6. selectric/OCR/typesetter	before typesetting	handwritten and or typewritten corrections on OCR document.

Ease of Operation

The potential for phototypesetting success rests most in the input operation. Almost every major factor influencing the quality of the output has as its basis the proper input of keyboarded information. As has been stated, typographic coding (mark-up) may be a separate operation, or may be a responsibility of the keyboard operator. Regardless of who assumes the mark-up function, it is the keyboard operator who most directly determines the accuracy of input and sometimes the overall appearance of the output. Additionally, in some cases the operator is responsible for line-ending decisions, hyphenation breaks, spacing and positioning judgments, and typeface and size selections.

Keyboarding, then, is not synonymous with typing, nor with word processing. Although all three require similar manual skills, phototypesetting is more complex; and unlike typing or initial word processing entry, there is a time lag between input and output. This time lag means that the operator must be able to visualize input before it occurs in order to reduce or eliminate the necessity for gross revisions.

Although typesetting skills are more involved than typing skills, they are not necessarily difficult. Certainly the speed of an input operator is dependent upon typing speed; but the typographic skills and technical information necessary to operate most phototypesetters are within the grasp of most people, regardless of their lack of typesetting experience.

Editing

Editing has two meanings, depending in large part on whether it is being performed by a person or a machine. The person, or editor, alters copy to conform to style, to clarify content, and to fit space requirements. The machine, on the other hand, is a device for assembling copy by rearrangement; similar in a sense, to the way that motion picture film is cut and spliced to achieve continuity.

There are a number of ways in which copy can be edited within a phototypesetting system (see Exhibit 8). The most specialized means is by the VDT, or editing terminal. The VDT is comprised of a CRT screen with dedicated keypads to direct the electronic movement of text. Certain direct-entry phototypesetters also have editing capabilities, but the presence of a CRT screen should not automatically be interpreted as identifying an editing terminal. The screen may merely provide a visual display of keyboarded information and with record/playback, may only permit correcting rather than editing functions.

Exhibit 8. Editing Functions and their Meanings

Function	Meaning
deletion	elimination of specified characters, words, lines, paragraphs, or other text blocks
insertion	addition of virtually unlimited text, from single characters to entire copy blocks
re-write	writing over existing copy to replace character-for-character with revisions
home	replaces cursor (location marker) to top left corner of screen
cursor keys	(cursor up/down/left/right) moves cursor in any compass direction
scroll up/down	lines held in memory are moved up or down screen

Author's Alterations

In newspaper newsrooms it is becoming increasingly common for reporters to input their own stories. The advantages to this should be obvious by now. In most other typesetting situations, however, the input operation is handled by someone other than the information originator. For this reason, it is often necessary that a typeset proof or facsimile be returned to the source for review and revision.

There seems to be some dynamic force which compels authors to change copy once they see it typeset. It may be that the author realizes that his or her words have reached their ultimate and final form, or perhaps, that the passage of time has created some new thoughts and altered some old ones. Regardless, author's alterations (A.A.'s) are a certain part of the typesetting process. Even if the typesetting system can deliver an accurate and timely product, there is absolutely no guarantee that external forces will not react adversely and return the product for massive revision. Knowledge of these possibilities should suggest to the reader that a well-planned phototypesetting system must have a record/playback capability along with the facility to edit.

Proofreading

A proof is an examination copy of typeset material used for marking corrections and revisions. Proofreading, then, is the activity of examining proofs for errors in either form or content, or both. Whether proofreading is the full-time responsibility of many people, or the part-time responsibility of one, it is an absolutely essential function for all typesetting installations. This step is usually the last checkpoint before committing typeset material to the final steps of graphic reproduction. See Exhibit 9.

Exhibit 9. Standard Proofreader's Marks

Punctuation Marks

period	⊙
comma	⌃
semicolon	⊙
apostrophe	✔
quotation marks	✔ ✔
exclamation point	!/
hyphen	-/
parentheses	(/)
brackets	[/]

Deletions

delete, take out	γ

Insertions

letterspace	ℓ/ʌ
insert space	#
em quad	□

Changes

wrong font	wf/
transpose	tr

Typographic Style

set in capitals	*caps*
set in lower case	*(lc)*
set in small caps	*sm caps*
set in roman	*rom.*
set in italic	*ital.*
set in lightface	*lf*
set in boldface	*bf*

Spacing and Line spacing

increase linespace	*lead* <
close-up, remove space	⌒
equal space	*eq* #

Positioning

move to right	]
move to left	[
move lower	⎵
move higher	⎴
straighten line	⹀
begin paragraph	¶
no paragraph	*no* ¶

Miscellaneous

let stand	*stet*
ok with corrections	*ok w/c*
ok as corrected	*ok a/c*

Record/Playback

Proofreading, author's alterations, editorial changes, and other unpredictable circumstances, all work to necessitate some revision of original input. The ease and efficiency by which revisions are handled is predicated upon whether the original input was captured on some form of storage media, and can be replayed and altered, or if all changes must be rekeyboarded. These, then, are the reasons for having record/playback capability — to avoid redundant keyboarding, to reduce cutting and pasting by outputting clean copy, to reduce turnaround time, to increase the productivity of the operator(s), and to retain work on a storage medium for future use.

The record/playback option comes in a variety of sizes and flavors. In its simplest (plain vanilla) form it is an add-on option to a direct-entry phototypesetter. The media which is produced may be read on the self-contained reader or may be read on an off-line VDT. In its most basic form such a record/playback option usually performs only the most basic correction functions, utilizing whatever character display that the phototypesetter has. Utilizing the same media on a VDT permits the full power of the terminal to massage the text into whatever form is needed.

Many functions of the VDT are incorporated into a category of sophisticated direct-entry phototypesetters (some call photo-wordprocessors) which are used for original entry, subsequent revisions, and ultimate typesetting.

I/O systems use off-line keyboards which by their very nature produce a storage medium. In such a configuration, a VDT can be used as middleman between input and output. In other cases, the original input may be directly from an editing keyboard. See Exhibit 3 for other configurations.

Media

The idea for typesetting media dates back to 1883, when Tolbert Lanston, inventor of the Monotype, made his first sketches of a keyboard utilizing a perforated ribbon of paper. These sketches became the basis for the Monotype system employing a separate keyboard (off-line) and caster. It was not until 1926 that Walter Morey proposed the same method for operating linecasting machines (Linotype, Intertype). His idea involved using existing keyboard perforators used for wire communication purposes. The system, which operated from distant locations, was named Teletypesetter, and the code it used was named TTS. The TTS code was adopted for use early in the development of phototypesetting and it appears in tangible form as a series of either six or eight perforations across the width of a paper tape.

Today there are both perforated and magnetic media available for use on appropriately equipped phototypesetters. See Exhibit 10.

Exhibit 10. Phototypesetting Recording Media

Media	Form	Advantages	Disadvantages
Paper Tape	1000' or longer roll of paper, reinforced, or mylar tape. 7/8" for 6 level, 1" for 8 level. Variety of colors. Approximately 120,000 characters per roll.	Can be physically filed to suit need. Can be color coded to distinguish job, operator, or machine.	Serial storage, length of tape must be searched to locate successive data. Can be easily damaged. Not reuseable. Relatively expensive. Bulky and cumbersome.
Magnetic Cassette	Phillips type cassette Stores approx. 90,000 char.	Rigid construction safeguards contents. Relatively small. Easily handled and filed. Reuseable.	Serial storage, see above. Data is invisible. Revisions must be made on a second cassette. Sensitive to mag. fields.
Mini Floppy Disk	5" square, flexible housing. Storage capacity approx. 100,000 characters.	Random access. Storage in easily located files. Easy to store, file, handle. Reuseable.	Requires care when handling. Sensitive to magnetic fields
Floppy Disk	8" square flexible housing. Storage capacity up to 300,000 characters.	Random access. Large storage in easily located files. Easy to store, file, handle. Reuseable.	Easily damaged by misuse or abuse. Subject to magnetic fields.

Disk notations:

"Double density": data is compacted to permit twice the data in the same space.
"Flippy" (dual sided): double sided floppy. Recorded on both sides by a dual head drive.
"sector": a fixed length subdivision of the disk used to identify data storage positions.

IV.

"How is a phototypesetting system evaluated?"

Prior to making a financial commitment to equipment, but after surveying in-house typesetting needs (see Appendix I), and visiting a representative sample of existing installations, an evaluation of likely machine choices can begin. The evaluation may be an informal list of necessary capabilities, a precise set of specifications, or something in between. In any case, and to whatever degree, some consistent evaluation scheme should be used as a relative measure of the fitness of each machine to the purpose for which it is being considered.

Most often, the only meaningful measure of evaluation is one of comparison, namely comparing machine A to machine B on the basis of a stated set of criteria. This, of course, is subjective, since different observers having different backgrounds, prejudices, and needs will rate machines in quite different ways. However, so long as a single rater is involved in the process the question of bias is not really a problem since, in any isolated case, the bias should reflect the needs of the individual (assuming it is applied in an intelligent way).

How then to look at equipment and know what you're looking at? The process of doing so is certainly an educational one, and it begins, as has been said before, by doing homework; that is, by having a clear understanding of the present and future typesetting needs of the organization (see Appendix II). The needs of the organization are the single most effective means of defining the user profile—a graphic representation of what the proposed system must accomplish (see Exhibit 11).

Exhibit 11: User Profile/Comparison Chart

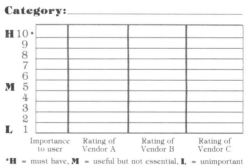

Category:_____

| | Importance to user | Rating of Vendor A | Rating of Vendor B | Rating of Vendor C |

*H = must have, M = useful but not essential, L = unimportant

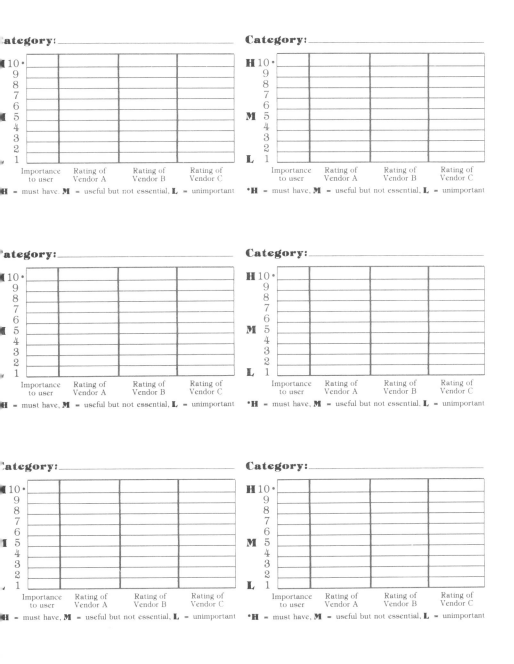

Category: _____

	10 ·			
	9			
	8			
	7			
	6			
	5			
	4			
	3			
	2			
	1			
	Importance to user	Rating of Vendor A	Rating of Vendor B	Rating of Vendor C

H = must have, **M** = useful but not essential, **L** = unimportant

Category: _____

	10 ·			
H	10 ·			
	9			
	8			
	7			
	6			
M	5			
	4			
	3			
	2			
L	1			
	Importance to user	Rating of Vendor A	Rating of Vendor B	Rating of Vendor C

·**H** = must have, **M** = useful but not essential, **L** = unimportant

Category: _____

	10 ·			
	9			
	8			
	7			
	6			
	5			
	4			
	3			
	2			
	1			
	Importance to user	Rating of Vendor A	Rating of Vendor B	Rating of Vendor C

H = must have, **M** = useful but not essential, **L** = unimportant

Category: _____

	10 ·			
H	10 ·			
	9			
	8			
	7			
	6			
M	5			
	4			
	3			
	2			
L	1			
	Importance to user	Rating of Vendor A	Rating of Vendor B	Rating of Vendor C

·**H** = must have, **M** = useful but not essential, **L** = unimportant

Category: _____

	10 ·			
	9			
	8			
	7			
	6			
	5			
	4			
	3			
	2			
	1			
	Importance to user	Rating of Vendor A	Rating of Vendor B	Rating of Vendor C

H = must have, **M** = useful but not essential, **L** = unimportant

Category: _____

	10 ·			
H	10 ·			
	9			
	8			
	7			
	6			
M	5			
	4			
	3			
	2			
L	1			
	Importance to user	Rating of Vendor A	Rating of Vendor B	Rating of Vendor C

·**H** = must have, **M** = useful but not essential, **L** = unimportant

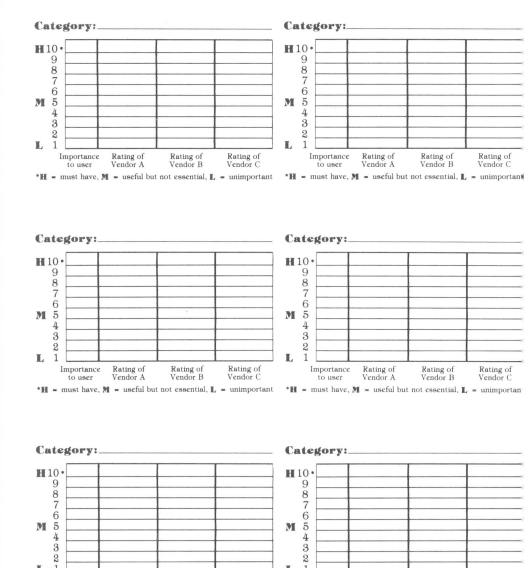

Suggested Categories:

Line length maximum = _____
Line spacing range = _____ to _____
Line spacing increments = _____
Typeface availability (specific designs)

_____

_____

_____

_____

_____

Typefaces needed on-line = _____
Sizes needed on-line = _____
Need for pi (unusual) characters (specify)

____ ____ ____ ____ ____ ____ ____

Type sizes on-line = _____
Type size range = _____ to _____
Formatting capability
Hyphenation (availability, reliability)
Character array (layout)
Tabs (number, kinds, ease of use)
Kerning/letterspacing
Record/Playback
Correction techniques
Editing
Speed (_____lines/minute)
Modularity
Service
Storage capacity (memory, media, expandable)
Length of average job = _____ (specify units)

Instructions: Enter the names of categories considered most important in equipment selection above each graph. Shade in the relative importance of each item to the user. Note the numerical rating for each category and total them. Evaluate equipment from different vendors, or different models from the same vendor and note the numerical rating of each. The overall totals (user needs vs. vendor ratings) provide a GROSS comparison of the relative suitability of the devices evaluated.

Next, on a separate sheet of paper form three columns. In the first, rank each category according to its importance (score). In the second list the scores of one vendor, or of a single machine from one vendor, opposite the appropriate category rank. Multiply each vendor score by the corresponding user rating, filling the appropriate location in the third column, and total the third column. This procedure should be repeated for all vendors and/or machines evaluated. The user listings, each multiplied times itself and totalled may be used as an absolute perfect score for comparison purposes. These total scores show in a relative way how one vendor or one machine model meets the needs considered most important to the user.

Quality

Equipment quality is a many-faceted subject encompassing such diverse things as:

- ✓ the presence of required functions
- ✓ the reliability of the electronics
- ✓ the flexibility of the programming
- ✓ the durability of the hardware
- ✓ the modularity of the design
- ✓ the compatibility with complementary and competing devices
- ✓ the serviceability of the components
- ✓ the maintainability of the system volume
- ✓ the ease of operation
- ✓ the accessability of functional controls
- ✓ the physical attributes of the typeset output

Some of these items are difficult, if not impossible to evaluate in any meaningful way, especially on an informal basis. The problem is further compounded by the vague notions and blatant misimpressions which both buyers and sellers have about the subject of quality.

It is beyond the scope of this book to launch into an in-depth study of all of the aspects of quality,* but there are some details which should be discussed, primarily under the topic of "the physical attributes of the typeset output."

The output, is after all, the final product of the typesetting system — the tangible form of a set of decisions, processes, and activities, usually requiring the combined talents of many people. From a quality standpoint, the output may be evaluated in terms of its macro-form (layout, design, page position) and/or its micro-form (individual character units).

The macro-form is solely dependent upon human decisions involved in the choices and sizes of typefaces, the length and depth of copy blocks, and the use of space and position. This aspect of quality resides with the user and is completely flexible within the limitations of the output device. The micro-form, on the other hand, is, to a large degree, engineered into the photo unit. It is the result of a combination of optics, image master(s),† escape-

---

*See "Practical Control of Phototypographic Quality", Michael L. Kleper (Rochester, 1978).

†Image master quality is not only the sharpness of the character images themselves but also the trueness of the character forms to their original design.

ment mechanisms, and electronic controls. The typographic characters which result are evaluated on the basis of the following:

sharpness: the detail of the character outline, i.e. the absence of an image fuzziness or out-of-focus condition.

alignment: the near-perfect horizontal positioning of characters along a line length. Even minute variability in this dimension is obvious to the unaided eye.

contrast: the proper exposure to light (and subsequent processing), yielding characters of the correct weight.

trueness to size: the precise correspondence of character images to their stated sizes.

uniformity: the exact match of character attributes over a predetermined period of time.

Speed

Phototypesetting machines are frequently evaluated on the basis of their ability to produce galleys of type. The word "galley" is borrowed from metal typesetting terminology where it means a flat metal tray used to store composed type. In a phototypesetting context, a galley is considered to be a length or section of processed output. The speed with which galleys are composed is usually stated in terms of characters per second (cps) or lines per minute (lpm). Characters per second is a deceptive measurement since it is dependent upon the size of the type being set: the larger the type, the fewer characters per second. Lines per minute is usually considered to be standard newspaper format, 8 to 9 point type on a 10- to 11- pica measure. Only when the point size and measure are known can the speed of one machine be compared to another. Also, frequent changes in point size and typeface substantially contribute to decreasing the speed of the machine.

Newspaper lines per minute range from 6 to well over 100, with CRT machines setting up to 4000 and more. The high speed of most CRT machines has brought the introduction of a new speed descriptor: pages per minute (ppm).

Knowing the number of characters per second, the characters per minute may be determined by multiplying by 60.

Characters per minute = characters per second × 60

Since the average word measures five letters plus one space (in phototypesetting a space is a nonexposed escapement), the words per minute may be found by dividing the characters per minute by 6.

Words per minute = characters per minute ÷ 6

The characters per hour is simply 60 times the characters per minute.

Characters per hour = characters per minute × 60

Assuming an 8 point type size on an 11 pica measure with approximately 30 characters per line, the lines per minute may be determined by dividing the characters per minute by 30.

Lines per minute = characters per minute ÷ 30

Finally, lines per hour may be found by multiplying lines per minute by 60.

Lines per hour = lines per minute × 60

Speed, although a useful measure of potential productivity, can be misleading when it is applied in practice. Most typesetting machines offer great flexibility in producing a variety of sizes and faces and are therefore not typically used for the standard newspaper format. The manner in which a machine is directed to perform a lens change, typeface change, line measure change, and so on impacts greatly on the overall processing speed, which is called "throughput."

Throughput speed is the result of job variables reacting with the rated machine speed. Size changes are a good example of this. To change from one size to another may be a mere keystroke, but that translates into the movement of lenses which may, depending on their location on a zoom track or turret at the time of the change, require less than a second, up to a few seconds for each change. Seconds add up quickly and detain the photo unit from flashing characters in the time it requires to change parameters. This particular example has an even greater impact on speed when lenses must be changed manually. Additionally, the larger the size set, the more time required for horizontal escapement to accommodate each character.

"What additional support will the system require?"

Photographic Processing

Up to this point no references to a phototypesetting system have included the last step in producing useable galleys of type, namely chemical processing. Although the future holds great potential for dry, instant-image materials, most light-sensitive materials must undergo chemical processing. The manner in which it is accomplished is quite significant since it will have a lasting effect on the useful life of the galley as well as providing possible alternate uses for the processor itself.

There are, fundamentally, two processing systems in use. The first is a limited permanency system called "stabilization processing." It is popular because it uses an inexpensive ($700 +) roomlight machine and requires little operator control. Its major drawback is that stabilization galleys are subject to fading and discoloration after a number of weeks (usually in excess of six). So long as the type serves its purpose before the image degrades, it is satisfactory.

The second system is conventional processing whereby the image is rendered more or less permanent. Resin coated (RC) paper, or typesetting film, is used in this system, with the major drawback being that the cost of the processor is significantly higher (up to $10,000 and beyond). Large processors also typically require a darkroom on the infeed end, and also usually require plumbing and drainage connections. (See Exhibit 12).

Paste-up

Paste-up is an assembly process which allows the manual placement of typographic elements (headlines, captions, text blocks) in combination with required artwork and photographs for final presentation (usually to a reproduction camera). Even if the typesetting system in use is capable of producing area composition, it may be more expedient to assemble it by hand than to plan and produce it on the machine.

Paste-up begins with a layout, a sketch which indicates the required position of each element in the overall designated area, typically a page. After the elements have been gathered, an adhesive, usually a thin layer of hot adhesive wax, is applied to the back of each piece. Guide lines are drawn on an appropriate substrate using a nonreproducible blue pencil. These lines indicate placement boundaries. Next, work marks are drawn to show trim and fold locations. The elements are then positioned using either a T-square and triangle, or (with a translucent substrate), an underlay grid, illuminated from beneath (by a light table).

Exhibit 12: Comparison of Processing Methods

	Stabilization	**Conventional** (Including Rapid Access)
Processor Cost	Approximately $700, items such as circulating pumps, dryer, and stand may drive the cost up.	Self-contained table top models from approximately $2500 up to standard sizes costing around $10,000.
Material Cost	Stabilization paper (least expensive alternative)	RC paper — priced equivalent or close to stabilization. Typesetting film — 4 - 5 times more expensive. Offers many advantages.*
Material Characteristics	Limited permanency Adversely affected by excessive light, heat, and humidity. Subject to stretch and shrinkage	**RC paper** Extended life. More dimensionally stable. Lies flat. Ink receptive surface for adding ruled lines. **Positive Film** Highly dimensionally stable Exceptionally strong. **Negative Film** Highly dimensionally stable Exceptionally strong. Requires a reversal film processor costing in excess of $30,000. May also be achieved in some instances by use of duplicating film.
Chemistry Capacity	Usually one gallon or less of each of two solutions: Activator and Stabilizer. After the recommended number of square feet of material has been processed the batch of chemistry is dumped and replaced with new.	Usually many gallons of each of two or three solutions: Developer, stop-bath (opt.) fixer. A wash step follows the fixer. Chemical strength is usually maintained by replenishment rather than replacement.
Processing Control	Replacement of exhausted solutions.	Change in replenishment rate. Change in processing speed. Change in developer temp. Change in roller transport path. Change in solution proportion Change in chemistry batch.

*See "Positive Film Make-up", Michael L. Kleper, National Composition Association, 1977.

Some Final Thoughts

● Don't discard current typesetting equipment or channels of supply until the new equipment is installed and operating reliably.

● Consider the possibility of retaining your existing composition equipment for its possible use as a back-up for your new equipment, or to help during peak production periods. If the equipment is still useable, does the salvage value justify selling it?

● Get everything in writing—the full costs including shipping, installation, training, maintenance, and spare parts. Insist (within reason) on firm dates for delivery and getting the system up to a productive state.

● Be certain that the proposed site for the typesetting system is adequate in terms of square footage, electrical service, floor covering (avoid static-producing carpets), temperature and humidity control, lighting, telephone, and plumbing (if a conventional photographic processor will be used). Consider the traffic pattern, and try to eliminate all operator distractions within the environment.

● If training materials, including machine manuals, are available try to get them in advance of the installation. If they are suited to the technical level of the operator(s), require that they be read prior to the initial training period. Also, try to secure basic information for the operator(s) to orient them to typesetting in general. You might pass along this book for example.

● Some vendors offer self-instructional packages in addition to the traditional machine manual. Some of these are quite good since they use the equipment itself to help train the operator. Additionally, the package can stay with the machine and be used in the future to train other operators, or to refresh the original one(s).

● Keep up-to-date. The typesetting and word processing technologies are the most dynamic segments of two large parts of the economy, namely the printing industry and the greater business world. You will find some sources of further information in the appendices.

● Get the people who will ultimately be responsible for the successful operation of the typesetting system involved in the decision-making process. It is almost always easier to introduce change when the participants are aware of what the change is and how it will affect them.

● All typesetting systems require some consumable supplies. Anticipate your initial needs and have them on-hand before the equipment arrives. Items such as photographic material and chemistry can be bought in bulk at considerable savings. Also, consider adequate storage room nearby the system.

● Become aware of similar systems in your surrounding area (city, state, region). Many users groups meet regularly and some even publish newsletters, which are an excellent way to learn and share quite specialized information. The existence of like equipment in your immediate area presents the possibility of establishing a reciprocal arrangement whereby the emergency needs of both parties can be met.

● It is quite handy to have a telephone with a long cord in the general area. This simplifies long distance diagnostic service by allowing the caller to access parts of the equipment while talking to a service engineer.

● Job descriptions should be written for each job function required to make the system work. Forms should be devised to collect needed information. House style should also be established so that all work is uniformly handled, regardless of when it is input or who does the inputting.

* * *

Appendices

Appendix I
Planning Timetable

Appendix II
Organizational Needs
(Departmental Typesetting Needs Analysis)
(Input Source Analysis)

Appendix III
Equipment Vendors
(Phototypesetting Input)

Appendix IV
Equipment Vendors
(Phototypesetting Output)

Appendix V
Equipment Vendors
(Word Processing)

Appendix VI
Periodicals
(Graphic Arts)

Appendix VII
Periodicals
(Word Processing/Office)

Appendix VIII
Trade Associations
(Graphic Arts)

Appendix IX
Professional Associations
(Word Processing/Office)

Appendix X
Equipment Vendors
(Interface Devices)

Appendix XI
Media Conversion Services

Planning Timetable

Project to begin   /   /   to end   /   /   total time: hrs.

Function	Min/Max Est. Times	Actual	Plus	Minus	Running Tally
Investigating system options					
Evaluating equipment peripherals					
Defining system requirements					
Management approval					
Project development					
Data gathering					
Data analysis					
Decision process					
Management reporting					
Employee search/interviewing					
Preinstallation planning					
Site preparation					
Installation					
Training					
System break-in					

Note: Use this form for rough estimates. For more precise calculations copy these function titles adding those which specifically meet your requirements.

Departmental Typesetting Needs Analysis

Department†	Job Description‡	Current Typesetting Cost	Freq. of Revision	% Revision	In-house Capability (yes/no)

†Such as accounting, administrative services, advertising, art, audio/visual, communication, composition, computer, data processing, employee relations, forms control, graphics, marketing, marketing services, personnel, printing, proposal, publication, public relations, sales promotion, service, systems and procedures, technical publications.
‡by name, category, or job number.

Input Source Analysis

Input/Complexity†		Time Priority‡	Average Turnaround	%Revision
longhand	1 2 3			
shorthand	1 2 3			
machine dictation	1 2 3			
typewritten	1 2 3			
other	1 2 3			

† 1 - simple (straight matter)
  2 - average (occasional size, face changes)
  3 - difficult (tabular, frequent size, face changes)

‡ A - most important (unrestricted allocation of resources)
  B - essential (rescheduling of existing projects if necessary)
  C - normal
  D - low (implementation time unimportant)

Appendix III

Equipment Vendors
(Phototypesetting Input)

ALPHATYPE CORP.
7500 McCormick Blvd.
Skokie, IL 60076

AUTOLOGIC INC.
1050 Rancho Conejo Blvd.
Newbury Park, CA 91320

AUTOMIX KEYBOARDS INC.
4200 150th N.E.
Redmond, WA 98052

COMPOSITION SYSTEMS INC.
570 Taxter Rd.
Elmsford, NY 10523

COMPUGRAPHIC CORP.
80 Industrial Way
Wilmington, MA 01887

COMPUSCAN INC.
900 Huyler St.
Teterboro, NJ 07608

COMPUTEK
63 Second Ave.
Burlington, MA 01803

COMPUTYPE INC.
P.O. Box 2080
Melbourne, FL 32901

CONTEXT CORP.
9 Ray Ave.
Burlington, MA 01803

DATUM INC.
1363 S. State College Blvd.
Anaheim, CA 92806

ECRM INC.
205 Burlington Rd.
Bedford, MA 01730

GRAPHIC PRODUCTS CORP.
522 Cottage Grove Rd.
Bloomfield, CT 06002

ITEK CORP.
1001 Jefferson Rd.
Rochester, NY 14603

HARRIS CORP.
Composition Systems Div.
P.O. Box 2080
Melbourne, FL 32901

HENDRIX ELECTRONICS INC.
645 Harvey Rd.
Manchester, NH 03103

ICS SALES & LEASING INC.
Suite 401, 919 18th N.W.
Washington, D.C. 20006

IMLAC CORP.
150 A St.
New England Industrial Center
Needham, MA 02194

INLAND PRINTING EQUIPMENT CO.
105th & Santa Fe Dr.
Lenexa, KS 66015

LEXICON INC.
60 Turner St.
Waltham, MA 02154

MERGENTHALER LINOTYPE CO.
Mergenthaler Dr.
Plainview, NY 11803

P.G.I.
16 Haverhill St.
Andover, MA 01810

REDACTRON CORP.
100 Parkway Drive
Hauppauge, NY 11787

REMEX
P.O. Box C19533
1733 E. Alton St.
Irvine, CA 92713

ROCKWELL INTERNATIONAL CORP.
Graphic Systems Division
2735 Curtis St.
Downers Grove, IL 60505

SHAFFSTALL EQUIPMENT INC.
Shaffstall Corp.
5148 E. 65th St.
Indianopolis, IN 46220

TELEX TERMINAL COMMUNICATIONS
2301 Terminal Dr.
Raleigh, NC 27604

VARISYSTEMS CORP.
80 Skyline Dr.
Plainview, NY 11803

VARITYPER DIVISION
AM International
11 Mount Pleasant Ave.
East Hanover, NJ 07936

XITRON INC.
814 Phoenix Dr.
Ann Arbor, MI 48104

Appendix IV

Equipment Vendors
(Phototypesetting Output)

ALPHATYPE CORP.
7500 McCormick Blvd.
Skokie, IL 60076

AUTOLOGIC INC.
1050 Rancho Conejo Blvd.
Newbury Park, CA 91320

BERTHOLD OF NORTH AMERICA
P.O. Box 430, 59 Willet
Bloomfield, NJ 07003

CAMEX
159 Lincoln St.
Boston, MA 02111

COMPOSITION SYSTEMS INC.
570 Taxter Rd.
Elmford, NY 10523

COMPUGRAPHIC CORP.
80 Industrial Way
Wilmington, MA 01887

COMPUSCAN INC.
900 Huyler St.
Teterboro, NJ 07608

DIGITAL EQUIPMENT CORP.
Continental Blvd. MK1-2 B11
Merrimack, NH 03054

DISCORP
P.O. Box 201
466 Kinderkamack Road
Oradell, NJ 07649

HARRIS CORP.
Composition Systems Division
P.O. Box 2080
Melbourne, FL 32901

ICS SALES & LEASING INC.
Suite 401, 919 18th N.W.
Washington, DC 20006

ITEK GRAPHIC PRODUCTS
Itek Corporation
1001 Jefferson Road
Rochester, NY 14603

INFORMATION INTERNATIONAL INC.
5933 Slauson Ave.
Culver City, CA 90230

LOGICON-INTERCOMP
P.O. Box 2933
24225 Garnier St.
Torrance, CA 90509

MERGENTHALER LINOTYPE CO.
Mergenthaler Drive
Plainview, NY 11803

MYCRO-TEK INC.
216 N. Washington
Wichita, KS 67201

OPTRONICS INTERNATIONAL INC.
7 Stuart Road
Chelmsford, MA 01824

QUADEX CORP.
241 Binney St.
Cambridge, MA 02142

RAYTHEON GRAPHIC SYSTEMS
528 Boston Post Road
Sudbury, MA 01776

ROCKWELL INTERNATIONAL CORP.
Graphic Systems Division
2735 Curtiss St.
Downers Grove, IL 60515

SYSTEM DEVELOPMENT CORP.
2500 Colorado Ave.
Santa Monica, CA 90406

TAL-STAR COMPUTER SYSTEMS INC.
P.O. Box T-1000
Princeton Junction, NJ 08550

VARISYSTEMS CORP.
80 Skyline Drive
Plainview, NY 11803

VARITYPER DIVISION
AM International
11 Mount Pleasant Ave.
East Hanover, NJ 07936

Appendix V

Equipment Vendors
(Word Processing)

AM INTERNATIONAL
Word Processing Department
1500 Wilson Blvd.
Roslyn, VA

AES DATA, LTD.
570 McCaffrey St.
Montreal, Quebec H4T 1N1 Canada

APPLIED COMPUTER SYSTEMS
615 N. Mary Ave.
Sunnyvale, CA 94086

ARTEC INTERNATIONAL CORP.
2585 E. Bayshore Rd.
P.O. Box 10051
Palo Alto, CA 94393

AVIONIC PRODUCTS ENGINEERING CORP.
Ford Road
Denville, NJ 07834

BASE, INC.
437 Madison Ave.
New York, NY 10022

BEDFORD COMPUTER SYSTEMS, INC.
Three Preston Court
Bedford, MA 01730

COMPTEK RESEARCH, INC.
445 Cayuga Rd.
Buffalo, NY 14225

COMPUTER POWER & LIGHT
12321 Ventura Blvd.
Studio City, CA 91604

CPT CORPORATION
1001 S. 2nd St.
Hopkins, MN 55343

DATAPOINT CORPORATION
9725 Datapoint Drive
San Antonio, TX 78284

DATA TERMINALS & COMMUNICATIONS
1190 Dell Ave.
Campbell, CA 95008

DENNISON MANUFACTURING COMPANY
300 Howard St.
Framingham, MA 01701

A.B. DICK
Information Production Division
2200 Arthur Ave.
Elk Grove Village, IL 60007

DIGITAL EQUIPMENT CORPORATION
Word Processing Group
75 Northeastern Blvd.
Nashua, NH 03060

EDIT SYSTEMS, INC.
23501 Jefferson
St. Clair Shores, MI 48080

FOUR-PHASE SYSTEMS
19333 Vallco Parkway
Cupertino, CA 95014

GENERAL COMPUTER/SYSTEMS, INC.
16600 Dooley Road
Addison, TX 75001

IBM
Office Products Division
Parsons Pond Drive
Franklin Lakes, NJ 07417

JACQUARD SYSTEMS
1639 11th St.
Santa Monica, CA 90404

LANIER BUSINESS PRODUCTS
1700 Chantilly Drive, NE
Atlanta, GA 30324

LEXITRON CORPORATION
9600 DeSota Ave.
Chatsworth, CA 91311

LINOLEX
Subsidiary of 3M Co.
3M Center
Saint Paul, MN 55101

MCM COMPUTERS, INC.
2125 Center Ave.
Fort Lee, NJ 07024

MICOM DATA SYSTEMS, LTD.
447 Saint Helen St.
Montreal, Quebec H2Y 2K9, Canada

NBI
5595 East Arapahoe Ave.
Boulder, CO 80303

OLIVETTI CORP. OF AMERICA
500 Park Ave.
New York, NY 10022

OMNITEXT, INC.
P.O. Box 2090
Ann Arbor, MI 48108

PHILLIPS BUSINESS SYSTEMS
175 Froehlich Farm Blvd.
Woodbury, NY 11797

QI CORP.
125 Rice Field Lane
Hauppauge, NY 11787

QUALTERM TERMINALS
453 Ravandale Dr.
Mountain View, CA 94043

QYX
264 Welsh Pool Rd.
Lionville, PA 19353

REDACTRON CORP.
1 Huntington Quadrangle
Melville, NY 11746

SAVIN BUSINESS MACHINES CORP.
Columbus Ave.
Valhalla, NY 10595

TRENDATA
610 Palomar Ave.
Sunnyvale, CA 94086

TYCOM SYSTEMS CORP.
26 Just Rd.
Fairfield, NJ 07006

VYDEC, INC.
9 Vreeland Rd.
Florham Park, NJ 07932

WANG LABORATORIES
1 Industrial Ave.
Lowell, MA 01851

WILLOW ASSOCIATES
766 York Rd.
Jenkintown, PA 19046

WORDPLEX
31829 West La Tienda Dr.
Westlake Village, CA 91361

WORLD INFORMATION SYSTEMS, INC.
17501 South Figueroa St.
Gardena, CA 90248

XEROX CORPORATION
Office Systems Division
P.O. Box 29466
Dallas, TX 75229

XMark CORP.
3176 Pullman St.
Costa Mesa, CA 92627

Appendix VI
Periodicals
(Graphic Arts)

AMERICAN PRINTER
Maclean-Hunter Publishing Corp.
300 W. Adams St.
Chicago, IL 60606

BOOK PRODUCTION INDUSTRY
21 Charles St.
P.O. Box 429
Saugatuck Station
Westport, CT 06880

BUSINESS FORMS REPORTER
North American Publishing Co.
401 N. Broad St.
Philadelphia, PA 19108

EDITOR & PUBLISHER
Editor & Publisher Co. Inc.
575 Lexington Ave.
New York, NY 10022

GRAPHIC ARTS BUYER
Advertising Trade Publications, Inc.
19 West 44th St.
New York, NY 10036

GRAPHIC ARTS LITERATURE ABSTRACTS
Graphic Arts Research Center
Rochester Institute of Technology
One Lomb Memorial Drive
Rochester, NY 14623

GRAPHIC ARTS MONTHLY
666 Fifth Ave.
New York, NY 10019

GRAPHIC COMMUNICATIONS WORLD
Technical Information, Inc.
P.O. Box 12000
Lake Park, FL 33403

IN-PLANT PRINTER
910 Skokie Blvd.
Northbrook, IL 60062

NEW ENGLAND PRINTER AND PUBLISHER
P.O. Box 597
35 Pelham Rd.
Salem, NH 03079

PHOTO TYPESETTING
Society Publications Ltd.
7 W. Halkin St.
Belgrave Sq.
London, S.W. 1 England

PRINTING TODAY
Northwood Publications
Elm House
10-16 Elm St.
London WCIX OBP, England

PRINTING EQUIPMENT NEWS
801 West Milford St.
P.O. Box 10820
Glendale, CA 91209

PRINTING IMPRESSIONS
North American Publishing Co.
401 N. Broad St.
Philadelphia, PA 19108

PRINTING NEWS
468 Park Ave. So.
New York, NY 10016

PUBLISHER'S AUXILIARY
National Newspaper Assn.
1627 K St.
Suite 400
Washington, D.C. 20006

PUBLISHERS WEEKLY
R.R. Bowker
P.O. Box 67
Whitinsville, MA 01588

REPRODUCTIONS REVIEW AND METHODS
North American Publishing Co.
401 N. Broad St.
Philadelphia, PA 19108

REPROGRAPHICS
United Business Publications, Inc.
750 Third Ave.
New York, NY 10017

SEYBOLD REPORT
Box 644
Media, PA 19063

TYPEWORLD
15 Oakridge Circle
Wilmington, MA 01887

U & LC (Upper and Lower Case)
International Typeface Corp.
216 E. 45th St.
New York, NY 10017

Appendix VII

Periodicals
(Word Processing/Office)

ADMINISTRATIVE MANAGEMENT
Geyer-McAllister Publications
51 Madison Ave.
New York, NY 10010

BUSINESS
College of Business Administration
Georgia State University
Atlanta, GA 30303

BUSINESS MONTHLY
United Media International, Inc.
306 Dartmouth St.
Boston, MA 02116

DATA MANAGEMENT
505 Busse Highway
Park Ridge, IL 60068

DATAMATION
Thompson Division
Technical Publishing Co.
35 Mason St.
Greenwich, CT 06830

DATA PROCESSING
IPC Electrical-Electronic Press Ltd.
79/80 Blackfriars Rd.
London, SE1 8HN England

EDITOR'S NEWSLETTER
Box 243
Lenox Hill Station
New York, NY 10021

INFOSYSTEMS
Hitchcock Publishing Co.
Hitchcock Bldg.
Wheaton, IL 60187

INFORMATION AND RECORDS MANAGEMENT
Information and Records Management Inc.
250 Fulton Ave.
Hempstead, NY 11550

INTERFACES
Institute of Management Sciences
146 Westminster St.
Providence, RI 02903

INTERFACE AGE
16704 Marquardt Ave.
Cerritos, CA 90701

INTERNATIONAL NEW PRODUCT NEWSLETTER
Transcommunications International Inc.
Box 191
Back Bay Annex
Boston, MA 02117

JOURNAL OF ORGANIZATIONAL COMMUNICATION
International Association of Business Communicators
870 Market St.
Suite 928
San Francisco, CA 94102

JOURNAL OF SYSTEMS MANAGEMENT
Association for Systems Management
24587 Bagley Rd.
Cleveland, OH 44138

MANAGEMENT WORLD
AMS Bldg.
Maryland Rd.
Willow Grove, PA 19090

MODERN OFFICE PROCEDURES
1111 Chester Ave.
Cleveland, OH 44114

NEW PRODUCT NEWS
Cahners Publishing Co., Inc.
5 S. Wabash Ave.
Chicago, IL 00603

THE OFFICE
Office Publications, Inc.
1200 Summer St.
Stamford, CT 06904

SEYBOLD WORD PROCESSING REPORT
Box 644
Media, PA 19063

Appendix VIII

Trade Associations
(Graphic Arts)

AMERICAN ASSOCIATION OF ADVERTISING AGENCIES
200 Park Ave.
New York, NY 10017

AMERICAN BUSINESS PRESS INC.
205 E. 42nd St.
New York, NY 10017

AMERICAN MANAGEMENT ASSOCIATIONS
135 W. 50th St.
New York, NY 10020

ASSOCIATION OF AMERICAN PUBLISHERS
One Park Ave.
New York, NY 10016

ASSOCIATION OF GRAPHIC ARTS CONSULTANTS
Printing Industries of America Inc.
1730 North Lynn St.
Arlington, VA 22209

BUSINESS FORMS MANAGEMENT ASSOCIATION
6204 North Delno Ave.
Fresno, CA 93711

EDUCATION COUNCIL OF THE GRAPHIC ARTS INDUSTRY
4615 Forbes Ave.
Pittsburgh, PA 15213

GRAPHIC ARTS EQUIPMENT AND SUPPLY DEALERS ASSOCIATION
Printing Industries of America Inc.
1730 North Lynn St.
Arlington, VA 22209

GRAPHIC ARTS MARKETING INFORMATION SERVICE
Printing Industries of America Inc.
1730 North Lynn St.
Arlington, VA 22209

GRAPHIC ARTS TECHNICAL FOUNDATION
4615 Forbes Ave.
Pittsburgh, PA 15213

GRAPHIC COMMUNICATIONS COMPUTER ASSOCIATION
Printing Industries of America Inc.
1730 North Lynn St.
Arlington, VA 22209

IN-PLANT PRINTING MANAGEMENT ASSOCIATION
666 North Lake Shore Drive
Chicago, IL 60611

INTERNATIONAL ASSOCIATION OF PRINTING HOUSE CRAFTSMEN
7599 Kenwood Rd.
Cincinnati, OH 45236

INTERNATIONAL BUSINESS FORMS INDUSTRIES
Printing Industries of America Inc.
1730 North Lynn St.
Arlington, VA 22209

INTERNATIONAL GRAPHIC ARTS EDUCATION ASSOCIATION, INC.
4615 Forbes Ave.
Pittsburgh, PA 15213

INSTITUTE FOR GRAPHIC COMMUNICATIONS
375 Commonwealth Ave.
Boston, MA 02115

INTERNATIONAL TYPOGRAPHIC COMPOSITION ASSOCIATION
2262 Hall Place Northwest
Washington, D.C. 20007

MASTER PRINTERS OF AMERICA INC.
Printing Industries of America Inc.
1730 North Lynn St.
Arlington, VA 22209

NATIONAL ASSOCIATION OF LITHO CLUBS
570 Seventh Ave.
New York, NY 10018

NATIONAL ASSOCIATION OF PRINTERS AND LITHOGRAPHERS
570 Seventh Ave.
New York, NY 10018

NATIONAL ASSOCIATION OF QUICK PRINTERS
528 South U.S. 1
Fort Pierce, FL 33450

NATIONAL BUSINESS FORMS ASSOCIATION
433 East Monroe Ave.
Alexandria, VA 22301

NATIONAL COMPOSITION ASSOCIATION
Printing Industries of America Inc.
1730 North Lynn St.
Arlington, VA 22209

NATIONAL PRINTING EQUIPMENT AND SUPPLY ASSOCIATION
6819 Elm St.
McLean, VA 22101

OCR USERS ASSOCIATION
10 Banta Place
Hackensack, NJ 07601

PRINTING INDUSTRIES OF AMERICA INC.
1730 North Lynn St.
Arlington, VA 22209

RESEARCH & ENGINEERING COUNCIL of the GRAPHIC ARTS INDUSTRY
1300 Old Chain Bridge Rd.
McLean, VA 22101

SOCIETY OF IN-PLANT GRAPHICS MANAGEMENT ASSOCIATIONS
666 N. Lake Shore Dr.
Suite 513B
Chicago, IL 60611

SOCIETY OF TYPOGRAPHIC ARTS
288 N. LaSalle, Suite 1205
Chicago, IL 60601

TECHNICAL ASSOCIATION OF THE GRAPHIC ARTS
P.O. Box 3064, Federal Station
Rochester, NY 14614

Appendix IX

Professional Organizations
(Word Processing)

INTERNATIONAL WORD PROCESSING ASSOCIATION
Maryland Rd.
Willow Grove, PA 19090

WORD PROCESSING SOCIETY
P.O. Box 92553
Milwaukee, WI 53202

Appendix X

Equipment Vendors
(Interface Devices)

ALPHATYPE CORP.
7500 McCormack Blvd.
Skokie, IL 60076

COMPUGRAPHIC CORP.
80 Industrial Way
Wilmington, MA 01887

DIGI-DATA CORP.
8580 Dorsey Run Rd.
Jessup, MD 20794

G.O. GRAPHICS
703 Massachusetts Ave.
Lexington, MA 02173

GRAPHIC PRODUCTS
522 Cottage Grove Rd.
Bloomfield, CT 06002

GTCO CORP.
10055 First St.
Rockville, MD 20850

INTERGRAPHICS, INC.
106 So. Columbus St.
Alexandria, VA 22314

ITEK GRAPHIC SYSTEMS
355 Middlesex Ave.
Wilmington, MA 01887

MERGENTHALER LINOTYPE CO.
Mergenthaler Drive
P.O. Box 82
Plainview, NY 11803

RAL DATA SYSTEMS INC.
7 Bridge St.
Glen Cove, NY 11542

SHAFFSTALL CORP.
5149 East 65th St.
Indianapolis, IN 46220

TYCOM SYSTEMS CORP.
26 Just Rd.
Fairfield, NJ 07006

VARITYPER DIVISION
AM International
11 Mount Pleasant Ave.
Hanover, NJ 07936

WANG GRAPHIC SYSTEMS, INC.
Executive Dr.
Hudson, NH 03051

Appendix XI

Media Conversion Services

AZTECH DOCUMENT SYSTEMS
575 Madison Ave.
New York, NY

CPT CORPORATION
1001 South Second St.
Hopkins, MN 55343

PROPRIETARY COMPUTER SYSTEMS, INC.
16625 Saticoy St.
Van Nuys, CA 91406

REPRODUCTION TYPOGRAPHERS
244 West First Ave.
Roselle, NJ 07203

SDA EQUIPMENT CORP.
71 West 23rd St. Rm. 1826
New York, NY 10010

TELESYSTEMS NETWORK
410 North Michigan Ave.
Chicago, IL 60611

TYCOM SYSTEMS CORP.
26 Just Rd.
Fairfield, NJ 07006

Names and addresses have been verified prior to publication.
Any changes, are, of course, beyond the control of the author and publishers.

Index